My Home

Stella Damarjati

My Home

My Home
ISBN 978 1 76109 504 7
Copyright © text Stella Damarjati 2023
Cover image: from Pixabay

First published 2023 by
GINNINDERRA PRESS
PO Box 3461 Port Adelaide 5015
www.ginninderrapress.com.au

Thanks to my husband Greg for his encouragement;
to my family and friends for their support;
to Julia Wakefield and Maeve Archibald for editing this book;
and to members of the Bindii Japanese Genre Poetry Group
for their advice on poetry and book publishing.

starry night
a heart full of hope
and dreams

Photo from Unsplash

our family

surrounds us as we
wait for our flight

we say goodbye
to the only
home we know

early afternoon

in the kitchen of my
childhood home

I chew
and savour sweet
sugar canes

monsoon rain

the child in me
screams with delight

as water streams
down pipes
soaking me

the smell
of last night's rain

lingering in the still air

origami boat
floats gently
on a puddle

Photo from Pixabay

my childhood home

we lie on the mattress
in front of the TV

watching
the adventures
of MacGyver

heavy downpour

I sit behind you
on the vespa

underneath
the rain mantle
going home from school

a humid day

clean bedsheets
hang on the line

the child in me
is running between
the folds with delight

leaving behind all
that we know

we wait

for the night
flight to
a new life

flock of pigeons
circle the house
morning flight

afternoon sun

the ice cream
melts and drips
down my fingers

a memory
of childhood innocence

Photo from Unsplash

my first
communion

I wear red and gold
my school friends
wear white

I feel out of place

Trust in life

To the child in me.
Remember smelling the wet earth after the rain?
You fold origami boats and place them
on a puddle of water, watching them float.
Remember your innocence.
Remember to trust in life.
You will be OK.

In the joy of spring and summer.
In the cold and wet winter of pain.
Trust in life.
You will be OK.

Remember to learn and grow
when facing life's challenges.
Trust that you will be OK.

And in your final breath:
Trust in life.
Trust in love.

she scoops

a handful of sand
and begins to create

the reality
of
her dreams

canola field
blooms golden yellow
noon sun

spring breeze

under the shade
of a sheoak tree

I breathe in
the scent of grass
beneath my feet

I see

the purple blooms
of jacaranda trees

there is beauty
and magic
here

Photo by the author

summer sunset

a blackbird
singing a song

this
simple gift
of joy

hourglass

time
is passing

I am
no longer a child
young and free

gentle breeze
pine needles scatter
on the bitumen road

autumn rain

I reflect
on my
identity

and the meaning
of home

an Australian flag
flutters in the wind
my home?

Photo from Pixabay

Two homes

I am an island drifting
between two homes
with no clear direction
lost as to which I call home.

I am an island drifting
between two homes
one a stranger, the other a friend
lost as to which I call home.

I am an island drifting
between two homes
living two different lives
one with a stranger, the other a friend
lost as to which I call home.

still dawn
dew glistens on green
rice paddies

red and white flag

of my country
of birth

I am a stranger here
I forget the words
to your anthem

Photo from Unsplash

Fireflies

I want to travel
to my homeland.
Go back in time.
Back to when I was a child.
I want to stand in a field
of rice paddies as the sun sets.
Wait for the night to settle
and the fireflies to appear.
Watch them fly and dance.
Feel the wind on my face.
Watch them flashing on and off.
Watching these ephemeral lights
float in the night's darkness.

travelling back
to my birth country

the familiar
sights
and sounds

of my beginning

childhood memory

the joy of
riding my tricycle

lap after lap
in your empty
back room

I listen
as you sing

a lullaby

reminiscing about a memory
of you cradling me
in your arms

childhood memory

a late-night show
watching shadow
puppets dance

and falling asleep
in your arms

Photo designed by pikisuperstar/Freepik

after the rain
a magpie's
morning call

summit view

the twinkle
of city lights
below me

my home
of twenty-eight years

golden sunflower
I lift my face
towards the sun

Photo from Unsplash

My home

My home.
I come from the smell of my mother's cooking.
I come from the taste of sweet sugar canes.
I come from the sound of heavy monsoon rain.
I come from the faces of my grandparents.
I come from the colour of brown earth.
I come from the home of my childhood.

Acknowledgements

on my way ed. ai li, December 2020: 'the smell of last night's rain'

nights ed. ai li, January 2021: 'a humid day' and 'red and white flag'

a time of wonder ed. ai li, March 2021: 'I see the purple blooms'

a shadow of myself ed. ai li, April 2021: 'spring breeze' and 'travelling back'

washed by sunset ed. ai li, May 2021: 'our family' and 'childhood memory a late-night show'

silence ed. ai li June, 2021: 'early afternoon'

wanderer ed. ai li, July 2021: 'summer sunset'

the sweetness ed. ai li, August 2021: 'hourglass'

raindrops ed. ai li, September 2021: 'afternoon sun' and 'she scoops a handful of sand'

The poems mentioned above are called cherita. The cherita tells a story in six lines and it was created by ai li. If you would like more information about cherita, please visit https://www.thecherita.com/

Echidna Tracks Issue 5, 2020: haiku – 'an Australian flag'
Echidna Tracks Issue 8, 2021–2022: haiku – 'after the rain'

www.ingramcontent.com/pod-product-compliance
Lightning Source LLC
Chambersburg PA
CBHW070340120526
44590CB00017B/2965